Just as I Am

Topical Bible Study
Written By: *Dana Poole*

Kamikaze for Christ Ministries

To Live is Christ; to die is gain.

Philippians 1:21

All Rights Reserved

No part of this book may be reproduced or transmitted in any form or by any means, electronic or mechanical, including photocopying and recording or by any information storage and retrieval system without the prior written permission of the publisher except in the case of brief quotations embodied in critical articles or reviews.

Unless otherwise indicated, Scripture quotations are taken from the

King James Bible version of the Bible

Kamikaze for Christ Ministries

A Ministry of *Lost Sheep Ministries*

©2015 By Dana Poole

What is a *kamikaze* for Christ?

The correct definition of the word *Kamikaze* is translated to *mean divine wind from the legendary name of a typhoon that in 1281 saved Japan by destroying the Mongol navy)* : kami, **divine** + kaze, **wind.** God lay upon my heart that there is no other divine wind like the presence of our living God working through His people by the power of the Holy Spirit. As it is stated in Philippians 1:21- To live is Christ....to die is gain. Just as that divine wind saved Japan from their enemy so can we be that in our own lives and the lives of others. A kamikaze for Christ is defined as an individual who is willing to invade the enemy's camp and defeat him with no regard to self. Their life is laid down with a reckless abandon for the cause of Christ, All for His Glory. All for His purpose, Yielded to the Holy Ghost, full of the Word of God, diligent, watchful, and always wielding a ready sword.

A word from **Pastor Bob Gibson**
President and Founder of
Lost Sheep Ministries

Dana is a godly woman who walks in great humility and integrity. She honors the Lord with her daily devotion to Him in every area of life. Her knowledge of the Word and her love for people is expressed in all she does. Dana's sensitivity to the Holy Spirit would make her an excellent candidate wherever she would minister. I highly recommend her. Dana is a wonderful speaker with a warm personality who also knows the Word very well and how to apply it. She operates very strongly in the prophetic with incredible precision and timing. You will be greatly blessed to have her speak at your next event.

Pastor Bob Gibson
Until He comes......
We will go

Dana is available to come and speak, and do seminars on the Bible studies or to simply minister the Word of God.

E Mail: poolend1@gmail.com

cell phone: 281.650.9932

Table of Contents

Introduction-   Page 1
This will define insecurity and reveal
the purpose for the Bible Study

The Lie-   Page 9
Insecurity is not who you are. This lesson will
address strongholds and mindsets and the lie that fuels them

The Truth-   Page 16
In this lesson we will begin renewing our minds and
receiving the truth about our worth and security in Christ.

Applying Truth-   Page 22
How to put into practical application the truth of the
Word of God in order to erase the lies we have believed
about ourselves

Being Secure-   Page 30
In this lesson we will learn how to be secure in who we are
in relationships, adversities, and in your purpose.

Resting in Security-   Page 36
This lesson will reveal that security is something we
should be resting in not constantly striving for.

ACKNOWLEDGMENTS

I give all the Glory to God
for teaching, delivering and allowing me to share this
path to freedom with others.

Introduction

What a great adventure we are beginning. I first want to acknowledge that there are many books written on this topic and I am sure they are great, however I have read none of them. I tell you this only because I want you to know that my perspective on this topic of insecurity is very personal and it comes from God's Word, the one and only authority. My journey to freedom from this life debilitating affliction was a very private and intimate time between me, God and His Word. It took several years, but my deliverance has been permanent and true. In fact it flipped the script for me by unlocking my potential and purpose in Christ. I have written this Bible study in hopes that others will find the same true and permanent deliverance in a much shorter time. This is not an informative book nor is it a "self-help" type of book. It is an interactive Bible study that you must do the work in order to gain the freedom that you desire. I use the phrase "permanent and true " deliverance because I do not struggle with it any more. You may ask, "Are there times when the old familiar thoughts, feelings and emotions come to me?" and the answer is yes. But because I recognize what they are and realize they do not represent truth or who I am, I can apply the Word of God which I have come to know very intimately and the thoughts and feelings of insecurity leave. They leave because they cannot thrive where the truth of the Word has domain. This Bible study will ask you to memorize verses, to dig into the Word of God, and allow the Holy Spirit to reveal areas of insecurity. This Bible study is *not* about giving you information about overcoming insecurity, but you must be willing to receive truth about how you may have allowed it to control you; to taint your thought processes and hinder your relationships. You must be willing to proclaim that you are not a victim no matter the hurt in your past and be willing to fight for truth and forsake every lie as it is revealed to you. You must be humble and ready to repent when the Lord requires it of you. You must be willing to allow truth to shape your perspective of yourself simply because that is what the Word of God speaks about you and that truth tells you how your Heavenly Father feels about you. You will gain such a sense of value, worth and confidence that cannot be shaken because the reality you stand on is His Word and it never changes! Hallelujah!

I will say several times throughout this Bible study that it is "simple" or that "deliverance is simple". Please do not think I take lightly the torment of insecurity, however I do believe with all my heart that deliverance does not have to be a long complicated process. It is as simple as receiving truth and refusing lies. The hardest part is finding the hidden places in our thought processes and mindsets where insecurity has hidden. That all depends on how honest you are with yourself and how much time and effort you put into studying the Word of God.

Look up in your Bible Psalm 107: 20 and write it out here.

_____
_____
_____

To truly understand this Verse in context we should begin reading in Verse 17-20. In these 3 Verses we see a group of people referred to here as afflicted because of their own doing and in their desperation they cried out to God and He sent His Word to heal and deliver them. The same thing holds true for us. Because of our desperate state of bondage to sin, God sent us Jesus. He sent us deliverance, wholeness, and completeness. It states in John 1:14 *"And the Word was made flesh, and dwelt among us, (and we beheld his glory, the glory as of the only begotten of the Father,) full of grace and truth. "* By these 2 Verses we can see that our deliverance has been sent and it is through His Word that we will gain it because Jesus is that living Word. His perfect, sinless life, His complete sacrifice and His loving grace make it all possible for us. As we read His Word and seek the truth about ourselves and His heart towards us, we will come to see and understand things about ourselves, if we allow it. His Word is our mirror. His Word does the delivering work and it is His Word that will reveal to us our own heart.

Look up Hebrews 4:12 and write it out here

_____
_____
_____

This is what Matthew Henry says about Hebrews 4:12:

1.) That is *quick*; it is very lively and active, in all its efforts, in seizing the conscience of the sinner, in cutting him to the heart, and in comforting him and binding up the wounds of the soul. Those know not the word of God who call it a dead letter; it is quick, compared to the light, and nothing quicker than the light; it is not only quick, but quickening; it is a vital light; it is a living word, **zon.** Saints die, and sinners die; but the word of God lives.

2.) It is *powerful*. When God sets it home by his Spirit, it convinces powerfully, converts powerfully, and comforts powerfully. It is so powerful as to pull down strong holds (2 Cor. 10:4, 5), to raise the dead, to make the deaf to hear, the blind to see, the dumb to speak, and the lame to walk. It is powerful to batter down Satan's kingdom, and to set up the kingdom of Christ upon the ruins thereof.

(3.) It is *sharper than any two-edged sword*; it cuts both ways; it is *the sword of the Spirit*, Eph. 6:17. It is the two-edged sword that cometh out of the mouth of Christ, Rev. 1:16. It is sharper than any two-edged sword, for it will enter where no other sword can, and make a more critical dissection: it *pierces to the dividing asunder of the soul and the spirit*, the soul and its habitual prevailing temper; it makes a soul that has been a long time of a proud spirit to be humble, of a perverse spirit to be meek and obedient. Those sinful habits that have become as it were natural to the soul, and rooted deeply in it, and become in a manner one with it, are separated and cut off by this sword. It cuts off ignorance from the understanding, rebellion from the will, and enmity from the mind, which, when carnal, is enmity itself against God. This sword divides between *the joints and the marrow*, the most secret, close, and intimate parts of the body; this sword can cut off the lusts of the flesh as well as the lusts of the mind, and make men willing to undergo the sharpest operation for the mortifying of sin.

(4.) It is *a discerner of the thoughts and intents of the heart*, even the most secret and remote thoughts and designs. It will discover to men the variety of their thoughts and purposes, the vileness of them, the bad principles they are actuated by, the sinister and sinful ends they act to. The word will turn the inside of a sinner out, and let him see all that is in his heart. Now such a word as this must needs be a great help to our faith and obedience.

I thought Matthew Henry said it so perfectly and it is of the upmost importance that you understand the power of the Word and the work it is ready to do in you. It will most assuredly do in you what you can not do yourself. It will complete in you what He alone has started. It will deliver you from what you have been hopelessly in bondage. Right now you must set your mind to be disciplined in the Word of God during this Bible study. You cannot deliver yourself from the complicated bondage of insecurity. It must begin with you right now giving the Word of God first place in your life. Not in a legalistic way. But in your heart you must give yourself to it because you know it is your path to deliverance; because you know it is powerful and it can do the work of victory in you. Begin a love affair with the Word of God. Do not just read it, consume it! Do not only study it, but memorize it. Ask the holy Spirit to give you a hunger and thirst for the Word of God.
Write out a prayer in the space provided asking the holy Spirit to help you.
_____
_____
_____
_____

Now let us begin by getting to know and understand this bondage of insecurity.

Insecurity is defined as- uncertainty or anxiety about one's self, lack of confidence; not confident or sure : not adequately guarded or sustained : unsafe ; not firmly fastened or fixed : shaky : not highly stable or well-adjusted : deficient in assurance : beset by fear and anxiety

Insecurity is a feeling of general unease or nervousness that may be triggered by perceiving of oneself to be vulnerable or inferior in some way, or a sense of vulnerability or instability which threatens one's self-image or ego.

There are many different dynamics to how insecurity came to be a problem in your life. There are other wrong mindsets and strongholds that bring about insecurity. Rejection is the main one. I have found that the two go hand in hand for the most part. The way they taint our self image and our thoughts is the same, the damaging results are the same and the healing and deliverance process is the same. In reality there are three areas that we will be dealing with in this Bible study: insecurity, rejection and low self esteem because they come as a set. I will keep it simple and address them all as insecurity and by focusing on the Word as your deliverer, healing will take place in all three areas.

We must learn to be secure in God's truth and that alone
We must learn that no matter what, we are accepted by Him
We must learn to gain our self esteem from God's truth not from people
And most of all those three statements should be enough, more than enough!

The memory Verses for this lesson is **Psalm 18: 1-2.** Write it out here from your Bible.
_____
_____
_____
_____
_____
_____
_____

Write these Verses at least 5 times to help you memorize them. Post them where you will see them very often throughout your day. Think about the truth and assurance that is stated in those Verses.

Now is really the hardest part. Looking deep into yourself and determining why you are insecure. I will list some possible causes that might help you pin point how and when this may have got hold of you. However you may be like I was and had insecurity issues all your life and you really may not know what happened to bring it on. That is alright. Healing and deliverance can still take place if there is not a starting place. Ask the Lord to help you with this. He knows all about you, far better than you even know yourself.

Causes of insecurity:
- persistent sense of being unaccepted
- a tragedy, death of a loved one, divorce
- poor body image- think you are ugly, birthmark
- feeling overshadowed by others
- life failures

fruit of insecurity:
- need to fit in and be accepted, need to be part of everything
- self-pity
- Need to control things
- inability to receive correction
- lust for attention, starved for love
- opinionated, need to be right
- feelings of worthlessness
- envy and jealousy
- fear of confrontation
- a sense of pride/self centeredness
- tendency to blame God for what you are feeling insecure about

This is not everything but it might help you pin point what the insecurity is in your life. What has it attached itself to your thoughts and mind sets? How does it affect how you think of yourself and others? The key to be free from this is to be able to recognize it when it is at work. It is very subtle and it sneaks in unnoticed if you are not paying attention.

Your homework questions will be very introspective. Please take your time with each question. Pray about your answer. Be honest. Also do not look for something that is not there. This is not about picking yourself to pieces trying to find something bad. Let the Holy Spirit search you. If you do not have an answer that is ok. You might be able to come back and fill it in later.

Homework

When are you the most insecure?

_____
_____
_____
_____
_____

Why do you feel insecure at that time?

_____
_____
_____
_____
_____

What are your fruits of insecurity?

_____
_____
_____
_____
_____

In what way do you expect to be different by doing this Bible study?

_____
_____
_____
_____
_____

What changes are you going to make in your life in order to allow the Word of God to deliver you?

_____
_____
_____
_____

What relationships are affected because of the insecurity?
_____
_____

How do you expect them to improve?
_____
_____
_____
_____
_____

When did insecurity begin operating in your life? (remember this also involves rejection and low self esteem)
_____
_____
_____
_____
_____

Can you think of a time when insecurity was not operating in your life? describe it.
_____
_____
_____
_____
_____

After reflecting on your memory Verse describe how it speaks security to your soul.
_____
_____
_____
_____
_____
_____

Look at this picture and what it says. Answer this question:

Jesus loves me just as I am; what is stopping me from loving me just as I am?

_____
_____
_____
_____
_____
_____
_____
_____
_____

Now write out a prayer below thanking the Lord for loving you just the way you are and ask Him to forgive you for all the negative ways that you think of yourself and for not loving yourself just the way you are. Be very specific in your prayer. Use the answer to the above question .

_____
_____
_____
_____
_____
_____
_____
_____
_____
_____
_____
_____

The Lie

The best and most powerful lie that our enemy, the devil, has ever told the world is that he does not exist. However, the Word of God tells us very plainly that he does exist and what his intentions are. Look up **1Peter 5:8** and write it out below.

_____
_____
_____
_____

I want us to look at the word *devour*. It is crucial that we fully understand what God is truly telling us buy using the word devour.

Devour- Greek word is Katapino meaning: Eat up, swallow or drown

So to really bring this home: Our adversary the devil is like a roaring lion looking for someone to eat up, swallow or drown in whatever lie he can get them to believe.

Think about it. The only weapon the enemy has is to present you with a lie and try to trick you and manipulate you to believe it. That is his only weapon. Now putting all of this in context concerning insecurity This is what we have:

You are not insecure. It is a lie, designed by the enemy to keep you from being who and what you truly are. somehow through circumstances of life you believed that lie. Once you believed it, then it becomes a mind set or stronghold that must be torn down. But the good news is Jesus brings truth to combat EVERY lie, He has the power to tear down EVERY stronghold and His grace can raise you up securely to be the awesome women of God He has purposed you to be!

Hallelujah, how thankful I am for my victory in Christ. How thankful I am that I do not have to nor can I deliver myself. The reality is my freedom has already been bought and paid for by Christ's completed work on the cross and His resurrection. I take great comfort that He is now directing me to truth, He understands my human weaknesses and I have the Holy Spirit to empower me.

We must understand what strongholds and mindsets are, where they reside in us and what lie we have believed to give place and power to insecurity in our lives. A stronghold is a more severe bondage than a mindset, however if truth is not applied to a wrong mindset then a stronghold will develop. However, the way of deliverance is the same. The individual with a stronghold has a more intense bondage and much more negative fruit from the lie.

A stronghold is- a demonic fortress of thoughts housing a lie that control, dictate, and influence your attitudes and behavior; oppress and discourage you; filter and color how you view or react to situations, circumstances or people

Mindset- a fixed mental attitude or disposition that predetermines a person's responses to and interpretations of situations. An inclination or a habit.

I will list examples of some lies that you may relate to. Put a check mark next to the ones that you have heard whispered to you at opportune times by the devil or you simply believe them about yourself or are trying hard not to believe them about yourself.

__ I am unlovable
__ not as good as everyone else
__ not smart enough
__ not pretty
__ no one loves me
__ fat and ugly
__ nobody cares about me
__ nobody wants to be my friend
__ not spiritual enough
__ no one wants to hear what I have to say
__ I am stupid
__ I make stupid decisions
__ how people treat me shows me what I really am
__ I will be rejected
__ I am not educated enough
__ I am poor
__ They are talking about me
__ They are just humoring me
__ They don't really like me
__ I am disconnected from people

I am sure that there are many more, however this is enough for you to begin to pin point the ones you have been battling or believing. Do you see the common element to all those lies? They are all about self. A self consciousness. Too much about I,I,I,I and ME,ME,ME. Where is God in all those self centered thoughts? He is not in them because they are not truth. Our enemy wants us to believe that everything is about us. He wants us to believe that we have to be good enough for God's love, he wants us to believe that we will never be good enough to deserve anything good. Thank you Jesus that freedom, victory and salvation are not determined by *my* goodness, but by the perfectness of Jesus Christ! The devil wants us to think that everything centers around us and what others think of us or how they perceive us. Which in turn causes us to constantly look at ourselves, pick at ourselves, and put ourselves down. God never intended us to be so self centered in our minds. All of those lies that we hear or believe are drawing our attention away from others and onto ourselves. God tells us in His Word how we are to conduct ourselves. Write out in the space provided the following Scripture. **Philippians 2:3-5**.

_____
_____
_____
_____
_____

I love these Verses. It re-directs us in our minds and brings us back to a place of humility where we are focused on others and following Christ's example. We can clearly see in this Verse that we must be humble, putting others first, esteeming others, exhorting others, encouraging others, being more concerned with how they are doing. This is the mind of Christ! We must accept the fact that being self centered and allowing those lies to swallow up our minds is very prideful. I believe that pride can be the road in for insecurity to begin to mess with us. Only you and God can determine this for your situation. Therefore we will stop right here. Spend some time in prayer and ask the Lord if there is an element of pride that you need to repent of. Being real in this area is the key to your deliverance. Write out what He shows you

_____
_____
_____
_____
_____

The lies that bombard us do swallow up our minds, taint our perspective and hinder our relationships with others. They can literally shut you down and it is then when we push people away to protect ourselves. Then we make best friends with self-pity and depression is not too far away either. Then the devil has us right where he wants us. I know it is hard at times to see that the lies, thoughts and feelings are not truth when circumstances seem to validate them, however, circumstances do not prove truth. Truth is just truth it does not need to be validated or proven. You must decide to be determined to allow God's Word to be the authority of truth in order for it to begin to change how you think of yourself and how you respond in relationships. Truth truly can make you free. God clearly tells us this in His Word in John 8:32 "And ye shall know the truth, and the truth shall make you free." I want us to focus on the last part of that Verse- *make you free*. I want us to define the word make in order to know the deeper meaning that God has for us in His word. The Greek word for make in this context is:

eleutheroo- verb to make free, set at liberty, from the dominion of sin, freedom from

another's control, liberate from bondage.

Wow that is amazing when we look at those definitions. God is saying to us that His truth is powerful enough to set you at liberty, set you free from the dominion of sin, from the enemies control, and to liberate you from bondage! Hallelujah, what a Savior we have! What great and awesome power He has made available to us through His Word. He used that same word 6 more times to express to us this great power. Look up the following Verses.

John 8:36, Romans 6:18, Romans 6:22, Romans 8:2, Romans 8:21, Galatians 5:1

We have addressed that with an element of pride we make ourselves too important and that can allow insecurity to get a foot hold. Now we will see that making people too important can do the same thing. We must stop looking to outside sources to gain our self-esteem, security and acceptance. People will always disappoint us and fail us and when that happens it is not a reflection of us it is an exposure of something in them they need to work on. In order to be free from this we need to stop making people more important than God. When we find ourselves needing validation from people, needing that encouraging word or compliment from others, needing to know if they agree with you, needing to know if they accept or reject you to the point that it constantly is in your mind, then you have made people too important. It is not that any of that is wrong, however when we do not get it and that "messes us up" we are in a bad place and our priorities are not correct. When God is the first place we look to for validation, affirmation and acceptance then we know, no matter what anyone else does or says we are accepted not rejected; we are secure in Christ; and we are so very important and loved by Him. So much so that He sent His one and only Son to die for our sins that we could have a relationship and fellowship with our Creator. Stop right now and ask the Lord to show you where you have made people more important than God. Write out a prayer in the space provided asking His forgiveness and stating you are determined to allow His Word to change you in this area.

_____
_____
_____
_____
_____
_____
_____
_____
_____
_____
_____
_____
_____
_____

The last lie or trick that we will address in this lesson is how people treat us past, present or future, is by no means a reflection of who we are nor is it how God feels about us. Look up Numbers 23:19 and write it out in the space provided.

_____
_____
_____

The Contemporary English Version says it so simply
Numbers 23:19 *God is no mere human! He doesn't tell lies or change his mind. God always keeps his promises.*

We must keep in the forefront of our minds that God says and has proven that we are extremely valuable to Him! We are worth it. Every bit! We are worth the great cost of His Son's life. Even Jesus Himself concurred. He walked this earth in the garment of humanity, laid down His life willingly to be our sacrifice; and now is our High Priest and Intercessor. Our worth is not defined by our works, whether good or bad, or plenty or few. It is defined by God's love for us which is greater than any human can comprehend. It is why we were created. We were created to be recipients of His love. Over and over in the Bible God expresses His love to us. The entire Word is His love letter to us. I believe with all my heart that God desires above all things that we, His creation, come to receive His love without reservation; for He knows it is His unlimited love that heals our broken hearts, tears down every stronghold and gives us a sound mind. That is why we cannot allow how people have treated us in the past, present or future dictate to us our worth, validity or security. To give people that kind of control, authority and influence in our minds and hearts is to say to our Creator, that His love and acceptance is not enough. Purpose in your heart right now that you will no longer allow people to have that kind of rule over you and you reserve that place for God and Him alone!

Your memory Verse for this lesson is **Psalm 119:45.** Write it out in the space provided.

_____
_____
_____

Write this Verse at least 5 times to help you memorize it. Post it where you will see it very often throughout your day. Think about the liberty that the Word of truth gives you and the commitment to seek His precepts.

Homework

According to the lesson what is the biggest most powerful lie the devil has every told the world.
_____

Do you recognize the lies of insecurity, rejection and low self-esteem that have been tormenting you or tainting your thought processes? If so what are they?
_____
_____
_____

What are the 3 main lies addressed in this lesson? (not the list)

1 _____
2 _____
3 _____

What do they all have in common?
_____
_____
_____

How important is it that you put God first before people?
_____
_____
_____

What happens if you fail to do that and people are more important to you?
_____
_____

What happens when we put God first ?

Why is it important for you to meditate on the Word of God every day?

According to the lesson what determines our worth?

Does that ever change? _____

Reviewing your memory Verse for this lesson, what does it mean to you and how does it speak to your soul concerning the liberty you seek.

After completing this lesson what has been revealed to you about yourself that you need to change?

For in Him we Live, and Move, and Have our Being;
Acts 17:28

The Truth

We covered many truths in the previous lesson. Those truths are the very foundation that we will build upon. I say that because if you cannot receive those truths as reality then you cannot truly be free from the bondage of insecurity. Therefore let's summarize the previous lesson.

How you feel or think is not representation of truth
BUT *it is evidence of what you still need to deal with.*
Everything is not about you
BUT *everything is about Jesus*

I am so thankful for these truths. They are the very foundation of all my thought processes when I am perplexed about something that may be going on with me. These truths are our life line to all other truths. When you know that your feelings can lie to you and your thoughts may not at any given moment be your own AND that everything does not revolve around you, then are you ready to receive the truth of the Word and apply it to every lie and get free from what is holding you back or pressing you down.

The truth is we must have people in our life. We are called to love people, to minister to them and represent Christ. So, people are important, very important. Our family, children, husbands are important, but not more important than God. Jesus set the perfect example of how to set our priorities regarding people. He showed great love, compassion and sacrifice while He walked this earth, however He did all of that to show us the love of God, not anything of Himself. We will look closely at Christ's example that is revealed to us in Scripture. Look up the following passages and answer the questions about them.

Luke 4:42-43
Why do you think Jesus went off by Himself?
_____
_____

When they found Him what was His focus?
_____
_____

John 17:1-26
In these verses Christ shows us His priorities. As you read this what do you see to be first and in which Verses is it expressed

John 5:19
How does this Verse show what Christ's priorities were?

Luke 2:49
Does His Father's business include people? _____
How?

I think it is very clear that Christ put the Father at the very top of His priority list and people were second. I did not see at anytime that Christ was concerned about Himself or put Himself above others or the Father. When we have more concern for ourselves than we do for our relationship with God and for people then we are off somewhere. Now let me make myself very clear here. We are suppose to take care of ourselves and not neglect what is needful for us to be all we can be. The best way to do that is by having a time of fellowship with God in prayer, fellowship with the Holy Spirit and fellowship with the Word! The only way we can walk that fine line between selfishness and self neglect is by being lead by the Lord everyday!

Ladies the bottom line is, if we are focused on our relationship with God, believing who He says that we are, walking in the purpose He has for us, putting the Kingdom first, and loving people for Jesus, then there is very little room for insecurity to get in there and mess with us. However it still does and our Lord knows that and understands it. I know that one of the things that we all battle is being way too hard on ourselves when we find ourselves feeling insecure. We beat ourselves up and tell ourselves that we know better, yet those nagging, ugly feelings hang on. When we do that we are working with our enemy instead of against Him. Jesus knew there would be days like these and once again we need only to look to Him and the Word for our comfort and guidance. Look up the following Verses and explain how they are truth when you are feeling guilty for allowing insecurity to bind you up

Hebrews 2:16-18, 4:15

Romans 8:1

1 Corinthians 10:13

I take great comfort in knowing that Christ is my advocate. He has experienced first hand everything I will go through in this life. He knows my heart and He knows what it will take for me to surrender to truth. At this point we need to look at some Verses and you will need to ask the Lord to show you why you cannot receive that about yourself. It is important to be specific so you will know what the real problem is. Think of it like this. You have a cold. Every cold is different so you have to determine what your specific symptoms are so you can buy the correct cold medicine in order to get better. That is what we need to do now. We must determine which truths you are not believing for yourself. Look up the Verse and prayerfully consider if you receive that truth about yourself. If you find you are struggling with that, use the space provided to write a short prayer asking the Lord to help you to see yourself in that truth.

Ephesians 1:6

Isaiah 62:5

John 15:15

Psalm 139:14

I love this last Verse because it covers everything. We are fearfully and wonderfully made. With great care, attention and effort God made us and fashioned us in our mother's womb.

With His very own hands and love He created us. He put within you, your personalities, strengths and weaknesses. How amazing is that! If there are things about yourself you do not like and can change them (within reason) then by all means change them. But do not do it because you hate the way you look, or because someone else wants you to change. The same with your personality. Remember God created you a certain way for a certain reason. Embrace who you are exactly the way you are because the creator of the universe personally crafted you and guess what He said it's good! As His women we must stop giving power to lies. Stop referring to ourselves as less than, not enough or not good enough. Start speaking truth to ourselves and each other and don't stop until it becomes a powerful truth in our life. We have been chosen for a great purpose, that makes a difference in eternity. Do not make light of that nor down play it as if it were nothing. Remember many are called but few are chosen! You are chosen to be women of truth! To make a difference in other people's lives. To Glorify the Father and represent Jesus. What a great honor and privilege. Yes you are good enough because Jesus was good enough. There is nothing left for you to do but to receive truth, follow Him and proclaim His love!

the last topic I want to cover in this lesson is, knowing and believing. It is not enough to simply know the truth. You must believe it in order to apply it. For example:

You have written directions to your friends house whom you have never visited. You *know* that the directions tell you to turn right at the stop sign, however you are not sure if it is the right way to turn because you have never been that way, but you do it anyway because you *know* from past experience that following the directions will typically lead you to your destination . On the other hand if you *believe* your friend has given you the best way to go you have no conflict even though you have never been there before. You *believe* you will arrive at your friends house by following the directions

Now we need to see the definitions to put it all together in spiritual context.

Knowing- to perceive or understand as fact or truth; to have established or fixed mind or memory of something

Believing- to have confidence in the truth, the existence or reliability of something, although without absolute proof. To have confidence or faith in the truth

Knowing the truth is not enough to be free from the lies of insecurity. You must believe what the Word of God says about you and the life Christ has given you by His grace and love. You cannot simply perceive the truth or even state the truth, you must have confidence in the truth to believe its existence and reliability without having proof . You must reach this point of believing so that when people and circumstances seem to validate the lie you can stand strong, not wavering because you believe the Word. It is in our believing that the truth becomes powerful in us changing our minds, feelings, and thought processes. it tears down the strongholds and wipes away the wrong mind sets. It heals our heart from the wounds of rejection and speaks confidence to our self-esteem. Consider this statement:

Only if one believes in something can one act purposefully

We must believe truth before we can apply it to our lives and walk in it. Take some time right now and ask the Lord to examine your heart to see where you stand in this area. Do you know truth or do you believe truth? Write down in the space provided what He shows you.

Search me, O God, and know my heart: try me, and know my thoughts:
And see if there be any wicked way in me, and lead me in the way everlasting.

Psalm 139:23-24

_____
_____
_____
_____
_____
_____
_____
_____
_____

Your memory Verse for this lesson is **John 15:16** Write it out in the space provided.

_____
_____
_____
_____

Write this Verse at least 5 times to help you memorize it. Post it where you will see it very often throughout your day. Think about how this Scripture reveals how special you are to the Lord!

Homework

Consider this statement: *I am a blood bought possession of the Lord Jesus Christ.* What does it mean to you and how does it encourage your self-esteem?

_____
_____
_____
_____

According to your lesson what was the order of Christ's priorities?
_____
_____
_____

Put in your own words why His priorities were set in that order
_____
_____
_____
_____

How will it help you to be guarded against insecurity if you pattern your priorities after Christ's?
_____
_____
_____
_____

In your own words what is the difference in knowing truth and believing truth.
_____
_____
_____
_____

How important is it to believe truth so that you can be free from the lies of insecurity?
_____
_____

Review the 4 statements on the first page of this lesson that are italicized. Put in your own words what that is speaking to you
_____
_____
_____
_____

Review your memory Verse for this lesson and in your opinion how does it reassure you of your worth in God's eyes?
_____
_____
_____
_____
_____

Applying the Truth

Here is where the action is and where the rubber meets the road. The real work starts now. We have looked at quite a bit of truth and laid out a great foundation to build upon. We know where the truth is, we know what the truth is and we know we must believe the truth for it to work in our lives. Now we will apply the truth to all those lies that give power to insecurity. We will take the weapon out of the enemies hand. We will allow the Word to change us, because we believe the Word and what it says. Hallelujah! We will first define what apply means. Look at the definitions

Apply- to make use of as relevant, suitable or pertinent
to put to use, especially for a particular purpose
to bring to action, use, employ
to put into effect

Now let's describe what we are doing with truth based on the definitions.

We are making use of truth because it is relevant and pertinent. We are using truth for the purpose of defeating the lies of the enemy. By believing truth we are bringing it to action to transform our minds and tear down strongholds. We are putting truth into effect in our entire being.

Ladies that is our battle plan and we will be victorious in Jesus Name!

The first step to applying truth is to capture your thoughts. Do not let the lie run rampant in your mind. Do not let your thoughts go unchecked. God gives us clear instructions in 2 Corinthians 10:3-5:

For though we walk in the flesh, we do not war after the flesh:
(For the weapons of our warfare are not carnal, but mighty through God to the pulling down of strong holds;)
Casting down imaginations, and every high thing that exalteth itself against the knowledge of God, and bringing into captivity every thought to the obedience of Christ;

We are told in Romans 12:1-2:

I beseech you therefore, brethren, by the mercies of God, that ye present your bodies a living sacrifice, holy, acceptable unto God, which is your reasonable service. And be not conformed to this world: but be ye transformed by the renewing of your mind, that ye may prove what is that good, and acceptable, and perfect, will of God.

We must capture the lie, arrest it, apply truth to it so that our mind is renewed in accordance to the will of God for our life. It is God's will that we are free and secure in Him; not battling wrong thoughts about ourselves all the time. He wants us free, functioning in our purpose and furthering His Kingdom!

Now let's get busy. On the next pages I will give you a Verse. After praying about it, I want you to describe the lie you have been dealing with that correlates with the Verse. Not all Verses may apply to you now, however you never know what tricks the devil might try to throw at you later. The purpose is to be proactive against the lies. The devil always has a lie to come against the truth. Therefore if a particular Verse does not apply to you right now, try to think of a lie anyway. Then you will be ready!! You may be thinking that this has you focusing too much on the lie, however I have come to realize that unless you know the lies AND the truth you are only fighting half the battle. When you are aware of the weapons your enemy is using it makes you a more effective soldier. Recognizing the devil's lies tells us which truth is the most important to focus on at that time. That is application of truth. Knowing the lie and knowing the truth that disarms the lie. The deeper you go in the Word the more powerful the truth fights for you. For example it is one thing to know Jesus loves you, but it is all together a different thing to know how much He loves you and how great His love is for you. Ok so here we go! I have used the King James version. If you would like to use another version, please do so.

Write a description of the lie in the space provided after the Verse

Psalm 139:14
I will praise thee; for I am fearfully and wonderfully made: marvellous are thy works; and that my soul knoweth right well.

_____
_____
_____

2 Corinthians 5:17
Therefore if any man be in Christ, he is a new creature: old things are passed away; behold, all things are become new.

_____
_____
_____

Psalm 139:17
How precious also are thy thoughts unto me, O God! how great is the sum of them!

_____
_____
_____

Romans 5:8
But God commendeth his love toward us, in that, while we were yet sinners, Christ died for us.

_____
_____
_____

Isaiah 43:25
I, even I, am he that blotteth out thy transgressions for mine own sake, and will not remember thy sins.

_____
_____
_____

John 14:12
Verily, verily, I say unto you, He that believeth on me, the works that I do shall he do also; and greater works than these shall he do; because I go unto my Father.

_____
_____
_____

Mark 16:17-18
And these signs shall follow them that believe; In my name shall they cast out devils; they shall speak with new tongues;
They shall take up serpents; and if they drink any deadly thing, it shall not hurt them; they shall lay hands on the sick, and they shall recover.

_____
_____
_____

Romans 8:38-39
For I am persuaded, that neither death, nor life, nor angels, nor principalities, nor powers, nor things present, nor things to come,
 Nor height, nor depth, nor any other creature, shall be able to separate us from the love of God, which is in Christ Jesus our Lord

_____
_____
_____

1 Corinthians 10:13
There hath no temptation taken you but such as is common to man: but God is faithful, who will not suffer you to be tempted above that ye are able; but will with the temptation also make a way to escape, that ye may be able to bear it.

_____
_____
_____

John 15:5
Henceforth I call you not servants; for the servant knoweth not what his lord doeth: but I have called you friends; for all things that I have heard of my Father I have made known unto you.

_____
_____
_____

Matthew 3:11
I indeed baptize you with water unto repentance. but he that cometh after me is mightier than I, whose shoes I am not worthy to bear: he shall baptize you with the Holy Ghost, and with fire:

_____
_____
_____

Romans 8:10-11
And if Christ be in you, the body is dead because of sin; but the Spirit is life because of righteousness.
But if the Spirit of him that raised up Jesus from the dead dwell in you, he that raised up Christ from the dead shall also quicken your mortal bodies by his Spirit that dwelleth in you.

_____
_____
_____

Colossians 1: 22-23
 And you, that were sometime alienated and enemies in your mind by wicked works, yet now hath he reconciled
 In the body of his flesh through death, to present you holy and unblameable and unreproveable in his sight:

_____
_____
_____

1 Peter 1:23

Being born again, not of corruptible seed, but of incorruptible, by the word of God, which liveth and abideth for ever.

_____
_____
_____

Ephesians 2:10

For we are his workmanship, created in Christ Jesus unto good works, which God hath before ordained that we should walk in them.

_____
_____
_____

Romans 8:28

And we know that all things work together for good to them that love God, to them who are the called according to his purpose.

_____
_____
_____

Now I want you to find or think of your favorite Verse that tells you about God's love for you. and write it out in the space provided.

_____
_____
_____
_____

Now you have to keep these Scriptures close at hand to be ready to defeat those lies when they come and they will come! This is work and it is not for the faint at heart. You have to be determined and more so than your enemy. You have to stand up with a strong resolve and proclaim , " That's enough. No more will I believe those lies. No more will satan keep me pressed down, hindered and suppressed. I have had enough. I will not be moved by what I feel. I will be moved by truth alone! " You must keep speaking out your determination to be free and speaking out the truth of the Word until it is what you believe. I do not mean that you "name and claim it" I mean you really work at it by capturing those thoughts, arresting them, sentencing them to death by the Word of God and walking in victory. Ladies, we are His. We belong to the King of Kings and the Lord of Lords with angels watching over us and are dispatched to fight for us when we wage war. Therefore, WAGE WAR! The truth is when you put these principles and the Word to work, seek the Lord with all your heart and forsake all pride you cannot lose. You can't help but be victorious. Your mind will change. Your feelings will begin to line up with truth and you will be amazed at the peace you will have.

Answer the following questions about these pictures or quotes.

Be your own kind of beautiful ♡

What is your unique beauty that God created you to be. It is something that is your own kind of beautiful. It is ok to think like this because you are giving God all the glory because you know it comes from Him and not of yourself. it can be anything. Physical, mental, spiritual, emotional._____
_____
_____
_____
_____
_____
_____
_____
_____
_____
_____

What does that statement mean to you and what is the opinion of your Creator.
_____
_____
_____
_____
_____
_____
_____
_____
_____
_____
_____

> Do you think God ever gets sad? Like, "What do you mean you don't love yourself? I worked so hard on you..."

What is the truth about the statement above. Can you think of a Scripture that backs up that truth. Hint it is in this lesson

_____
_____
_____
_____
_____
_____
_____
_____
_____

Considering all that we have been learning what would you interpret this picture and Scripture to mean. Put it in your own words

_____
_____
_____
_____
_____
_____
_____
_____
_____
_____

Due to the amount and intensity of this lesson I have not assigned a memory Verse. Take your time and go back over the Verses. Pick out the ones that speak to you the most. Put them in a place that is easily accessible. Get organized with your warfare, because I guarantee you satan is strategizing how he can keep you from being free. I will end this lesson with one last assignment. Write out a prayer thanking God that He loves you and accepts you just the way you are!

Being Secure

I am sure you have found that your battle with insecurity has affected your perspective in relationships, adversities/conflicts, and in your purpose/ ministry. You must come to a place in your own heart and mind that how you feel or think about yourself is absolutely irrelevant. You cannot have a positive impact on the lives of others until YOU get out of the way. In other words until you see it is not about you; you are essentially irrelevant. It is all about Jesus and He is perfect in every way and He lives in you! When insecurity is at work in a relationship through the individuals it can be recognized by extremes. For example one may feel dis- valued, unwanted, to the point it affects their own view of themselves. They are very jealous and feel threatened by other people. It can also be that the relationship is one sided. The insecure person has such a self centered mentality that they are a taker in the relationship and never give back. They do this because everything is about them and when that relationship does not feed their self-esteem any more they have no problem discontinuing that relationship and moving on in search of another who will flatter them and build them up. Either scenario is not good and is a place of bondage with insecurity at its very root. I have personally experienced both sides of those extremes in one way or another and I am confident I am not the only one. In the middle of those 2 extremes is perfect balance and the way to find that perfect balance is by forsaking the pride and put others first. Relationships should be give and take and we should never remain in a relationship where we are being belittled, put down and never encouraged. Also we should not be so needy that if we are not being flattered, complimented, noticed and encouraged that we walk away from the relationship leaving the other person wondering and exasperated. It is unfair to put an expectation on others (especially husbands) to build you up in certain area because you are insecure there. The truth is as long as you allow insecurity to exist, there really is nothing anyone can do or say to make that better. You must fight to be free. Our number one relationship that we should be focused on is our relationship with God. If we get all we need from God then what other people do and don't do won't affect how we view ourselves. Will people hurt us? Yes! They will disappoint and let us down over and over because we are all in process. However what they do does not change who we are. How they hurt or disappoint should never change how you feel about yourself.

The three areas that we are covering in this lesson are intensely close to our hearts and call for your utmost attention. One of the chief ways insecurity works overtime in these areas is comparison. The voice of insecurity manipulates you to compare yourself to others If you have experienced this you know it is torture. See if you recognize any of these torments:

> My home is not clean enough
> I could never do all that she does
> People don't like me as much as they like her

> I am not useful because I am not as young as other people
> I am not as educated as she is.
> What I do is not as important as what she does
> I don't know the Word like she does
> I can't pray like she does that's why I do not get called on.

Does any of that sound familiar? That kind of thought process is agonizing and is designed to alienate you from people; to make us measure our worth by comparing ourselves to others. When we get caught up in the "comparison trap" it opens the door to jealousy, self-pity, and defeat. This mind-set will hinder every relationship. We begin to have issues with the person we are comparing ourselves to and they do not even know what is wrong. If it is allowed to continue you will get a "punishing" type attitude towards that person. You will want to put them down in order for you to feel better. This is a horrible selfish place to end up, however most do not realize it. Because insecurity is insatiable, even when beginning to feel better than the other person, insecurity will not let go It will not make a difference. Insecurity must be exposed and evicted for things to start to change. It takes time for wrong thought patterns to change, however when insecurity is no longer there and truth abides in its place it makes changing light work instead of a heavy drawn out process. Ladies Jesus is our example and it is He we should compare ourselves to . We need to remember we are all in process and not one of us is perfect. We have to allow ourselves and others to be who we are in that process and only compare ourselves to Jesus and the person we were yesterday; striving to be a better person than we were the day before. We can be secure and be at peace in all relationships because God is working on us all. Look up Philippians 1:6 and write it out in the space provided.

Philippians 1:6

_____

_____

When we compare concerning our purpose (your vocation, job, career, raising children) or ministry it is like we are saying, " What God has given me to do is not good enough. I want something better" . We have to value what God has entrusted to us or we will never get anything else. Can you see the element of pride that is in the comparison process? It is that element of pride that allows that thought process to take place. The way out of that trap is to ask forgiveness for the pride. Take on humility that values the purpose that God has given and begin to learn from those who you think are better. Be secure that you are a work in progress. Apply truth to encourage yourself in the Word. Purpose to be an encourager to others. Stop centering your life around yourself! Embrace the Word, capture your thoughts, and experience peace. Accept where you are in growth as a person and as a Christian and work to be better than you were the day before. By putting these principles to work the torment will stop. The self-hatred and self-pity will stop. The relationships you have will be more fulfilling and have a positive effect on your life.

Before you go any farther pray and ask the Lord if you have any tendencies towards this comparison process. Ask His forgiveness for that and thank Him that you know He is healing your heart and mind in that area with His truth. Write down anything that He shows you or you can simply write out your prayer, in the space provided

_____
_____
_____
_____
_____
_____
_____
_____
_____
_____

Adversities and conflicts with others are a part of everyday life. We have conflicts and confrontations and how we handle them determines the outcome whether it be good or bad. The part that insecurity plays in adversities and conflicts is subtle. It may seem right, maybe even humble. It may appear you are deferring to the needs or wants of others, but it is not. Actually the insecure person refrains from saying, "no" or doesn't want to "rock the boat" or doesn't stand up for themselves, to assure that others don't get mad at them or look at them in a negative way. A person who knows who they are in Christ and has a healthy balance between selfishness and self-less-ness can say no without a battle with anxiety. This person can stand up for themselves and rock the boat if need in complete humility. Ladies remember whose you are and stand on truth when you rock that boat. Do not avoid conflict or adversity by being silent when your voice should be heard. When this takes place it promotes resentment and will hinder relationships. If you don't want Chinese food then say, "I would rather not have Chinese food". If someone is rude to you or huts you, go to them in humility and tell them they hurt you. You are supposed to do that. You are not being humble, or super spiritual by being silent. But when we go to others when we have been hurt by their words or actions it gives everyone an opportunity to grow. That kind of openness cultivates strong relationships. Letting others walk all over you does not glorify God . However when we believe the Word, stand in humility as a strong woman, it is then we show the love and strength of our God. Insecurity wants to keep you *under* people. Pride wants to put you *above* people. Neither create good relationships. But love and humility has you walking *with* people, equal with everyone because God loves and values us all the same. Thank Jesus!

I want address a subject that deals with mothers, past present and future. As mothers we cannot allow insecurity to use our past, present or future, mistakes against us. we will make mistakes in raising our children and we cannot let that become something that creates doubt and insecurity. I have experienced that and I can tell you that if you allow the voice of accusation and persecution to continue it will shut you down spiritually, cause depression and cloud your judgments and thoughts. Not one of us is or has been the "perfect" parent. Therefore I submit to you this simple truth, *"If you presented Jesus to your child, taught them about His love and salvation, then you did the very best any parent could ever do!"* If you apply that truth every time those thoughts and feelings arise they will begin to lose their power and influence. Remember the devil knows how to hurt us and if you let him, he will make you feel like you were/are a lousy mother. I battled this for years because I was so young when I had my first child. I was 19 and I had a very strong willed little boy. I made so many mistakes. However, I have since then asked his forgiveness and because he knows the love of Jesus, he graciously forgave me. I can see him being an over comer and not making the same mistakes with his own child. I have a great compassion for mothers and I am protective of them in this area. That is why I am compelled to put this process in this teaching. Stand strong all you Moms! The very best you can do is give them Jesus. Forget the pressure of perfection. That is a weapon of the enemy.

Your memory Verse for this lesson is Philippians 2:13. Write it out in the space provided

_____
_____
_____

Write this Verse at least 5 times to help you memorize it. Post it where you will see it very often throughout your day. Think about how God is working in you. It is He that causes you to desire to do good and because of that you can be secure. He has deposited in you a form of Himself to give you all you need to be an over comer. To break free from insecurity. No matter what His love and acceptance will never change. His desire for you never stops and He never gives up!

Homework

Why is it torture when we compare ourselves to others?

_____
_____
_____

How does the comparison thought process alienate you from people and hinder relationships?

_____
_____
_____
_____

In your opinion how do you expose and evict insecurity?

According to the lesson, who are the 2 people we are to compare ourselves to and why?

Explain the element of pride in the comparison process?

According to the lesson:
   In what way does insecurity want us under people?

   In what way does pride want us above people?

   Where does love and humility want us?

   How do we do that? *use scripture to back up your answer*

How do you stand up for yourself in humility and strength? How does that glorify God?

How does the memory Verse for this lesson speak to your soul and build security in you?
_____
_____
_____
_____

According to your lesson, what must be done for you to be the best mother you can be?
_____
_____
_____

Referring to the previous question, explain how that is truth? Use Scripture to back up your answer.
_____
_____
_____
_____

Referring to the previous question, what does that mean to you personally as a mom or mom to be?
_____
_____
_____

Where did you find yourself in this lesson the most?
_____
_____
_____

What steps are you going to take to expose and evict insecurity?
_____
_____
_____

Resting in Security

It is very clear that God desires us to know we are secure in who we are in Him. He tells in His Word about His love for us. He tells us we have victory over our enemy because of Jesus. I believe it grieves our Heavenly Father when we believe the enemy instead of His Word, when we talk negatively ourselves or put ourselves down. Ephesians 4:29-30 says it very plainly. Look it up and write it in the space provided.

Ephesians 4:29-30
_____
_____
_____
_____

Most of us read this Verse and think it is about what we say about others or circumstances and it is. However, it also means how we refer to ourselves. We have already determined that we are highly valued by God, how dare we talk bad about the very person He gave His Son's life for. Who are we to decide that we are not good enough when God Himself proclaims that because of His Son we are good enough. God went to great lengths to give us assurance, victory, salvation. He did what only could be done by Him to defeat our enemy and then gave us delegated authority over him as well. (Mark 16:17-18) Come on ladies, we have to stop fighting a war that has already been won. God tells us simply and clearly in His Word that it is done. Satan has no more rights to us who believe and have received Jesus.

Colossians 2:13-15 Amplified Bible
13 When you were dead in your sins and in the uncircumcision of your flesh (worldliness, manner of life), God made you alive together with Christ, having [freely] forgiven us all our sins,
14 having canceled out the certificate of debt consisting of legal demands [which were in force] against us and which were hostile to us. And this certificate He has set aside and completely removed by nailing it to the cross.
15 When He had disarmed the rulers and authorities [those supernatural forces of evil operating against us], He made a public example of them [exhibiting them as captives in His triumphal procession], having triumphed over them through the cross.

God has sealed us with the Holy Spirit and made us more than conquerors in Christ Jesus!

Ephesians 1:13
In whom ye also trusted, after that ye heard the word of truth, the gospel of your salvation: in whom also after that ye believed, ye were **sealed** with that holy Spirit of promise,

Romans 8:37
Nay, in all these things we are more than **conqueror**s through him that loved us.

God's Word is very plain. We have been granted, by the grace and love of Jesus, victory, power and life. Look up 2 Peter 1:2-4 and write it out in the space provided

2 Peter 1:2-4
_____
_____
_____
_____

Who do all those Scriptures describe? They describe you! A loved, valued woman of God who has been freely set free by a loving and gracious Savior! Purpose right now to be a woman of truth that does not fight wars that have already been won. No more wasting time on wrong thoughts and insecurities. No more speaking negatively about what God holds so dearly. Be a woman who not only knows and believes truth but rests in it as well. Because the truth is: You are completely and wholly secure in Him. You can rest all of who you are and who you are not is securely in Him. Nothing and no one can tear you down or make you less than. There is nothing else that needs to be done. Jesus already did it all. Rest in it woman of God.

Your memory Verse for this lesson is John 19:30. Write it out in the space provided
_____
_____
_____

Write this Verse at least 5 times to help you memorize it. Post it where you will see it very often throughout your day. Think about how the war has already been won. All that is left is for you to receive truth.

Homework

Do you see yourself in victory? _____ why? _____
_____
_____

How does the memory Verse for this lesson help you rest in the security of who you are in Christ?
_____
_____
_____

What does it mean for you to rest in the security of who you are in Christ?
_____
_____
_____

What keeps you from that rest?
_____
_____
_____

What changes are you going to make in order for that rest to become a reality?
_____
_____
_____

Describe in your own words what Colossians 2:13-15 is saying?
_____
_____
_____

How do you stop fighting a war that has already been won?
_____
_____
_____
_____

Describe what this Bible study has meant to you and in what way it has changed you

_____
_____
_____
_____
_____
_____
_____

Share with at least one person what you have learned in this Bible study. Write down what you shared and the person's response

_____
_____
_____
_____
_____
_____
_____
_____
_____
_____
_____

Write out a prayer thanking God for victory and your desire to rest in the security of who you are in Christ. Use at least 3 Scriptures in your prayer

_____
_____
_____
_____
_____
_____
_____
_____
_____
_____
_____
_____
_____
_____
_____

Father I thank You for each woman that has read these pages and I ask that You bless them. Speak to their hearts and minds all the truths they have learned. Let them not waver. Strengthen them according to Your power. Remind them often to rest. Give them great passion for Your Word and cause it to truly be alive. Call them deeper into Your love and help them believe You. Give them confidence to share Your truth. Smile upon them Lord, and make Your presence so very real to them. Let them not hang their head, but cause them to lift their head because of Your great workmanship in them. Keep them in perfect balance and make their victory assured in their minds and hearts. Quicken them if they begin to fall into old thought patterns and remind them that you understand their humanity. Cause them to never forget who they are and may insecurity never befall them again!!

In the mighty name of Jesus our Savior, our King and our Lord!

www.ingramcontent.com/pod-product-compliance
Lightning Source LLC
Chambersburg PA
CBHW060758090426
42736CB00002B/75